UNMASKING

POEMS AND THE THOUGHTS BEHIND THEM

To: Kelly,

Remember,
  You are The CEO of
Your life so hire, fire, and
Promote accordingly, Not
everyone deserve a front
Row Seat to Your life,
        God Bless
        Eric Kennedy
        10-11/22

Eric Orion Kennedy

CONTENTS

DEDICATION

I dedicate this book to Mary L. Wilcox, who opened her heart, family, and her home to so many of us who so desperately needed it. Through all of my faults, baggage, and disappointments, you never gave up on me. You are the reason I manage to survive so long through a life where it would have been so easy to use the excuse of my past hurts and treatment. However, you taught me to choose the path God has laid out for me. Although not easy, I persevered with your teachings and guidance. I proudly call you, mom!

God blesses you!

PROLOGUE

Live, love, laugh is a phrase I have been using for over 20 years. It is a constant reminder not only of my mother who has always urged me to live by the three Ls and not the three Ws.

The LS being, you guessed it live, love, laugh, and the three Ws being worrying, working, and whining. A concept that I'll explain later.

Live, love, laugh is also a reminder not to take life so seriously. You may think that it is silly to be reminded to live, love, and laugh; it should come naturally. I agree that these should come naturally. However, for many of us, we can get so engulfed in the world. To the point, we live a little less, and for some not at all. We love the wrong way, or not at all (as described in this book), and for most people it has become extremely difficult to find things to laugh about in their lives, therefore they laugh less and less each day. I thank my mom for engraving these three words into my mind, but most importantly, into my heart.

Now any time I sign my name to things I also include live, love, and laugh as my epithet. My favorite place to leave it is on my restaurant receipts. Ninety percent of the time, I get a positive response to it. I'm sure the other ten percent of the time is positive as well, even though I don't witness it for myself.

I've decided to title the prologue live, love, laugh as a reminder to all those who will read this. I sub-titled its poems and the thoughts behind them because I didn't want to write a book of just my poems. The poems were just the beginning of a thought I had on a particular subject. The pages that follow each poem are the continuations of those thoughts, and at the end of each chapter, there are questionnaires.

The reason for the questions is to stir up emotions and thoughts inside of you, with hopes to cause you to take a closer look at your life, and give you the opportunity, to be honest with yourself. I encourage you to take the time to answer the questions. You can answer them in your mind, but I strongly suggest that you write them down, meditate and pray on the answers.

This book also has a spiritual tone to it, which I hope will cause those of you who have a relationship with Christ to take it up a notch. It is also my hope that for those that do not have a relationship with Christ after reading my book it will excite your interest in wanting one. Happy reading and God bless.

Eric Orion Kennedy

CHAPTER 1

The pariah mask

It's not Halloween, yet I wear this mask,

It's a mask society has given to me.

A mask; I hope to take off eventually.

The life I'm living society considers wrong

Then they glorify it with movies, videos, and songs.

At very young age, This is what was taught you see and yet, as I part take you condemn me.

As I got older and in turn a lot bolder,

Some would say my heart has gotten colder.

Now, the drug and gang life is dangerously integrated,

As I now find myself incarcerated.

I sit here with time to ponder.

How friends are few, acquaintances are plenty. Fakes of both I now know are many.

To those who tried to point me in the right direction, I thank you. I've ignored your advice and made this lifestyle my occupation.

My soul continues to cry.

"it's never too late to change."

For the ones I love, I know I must try.

So behind this mask, I now smile, at a chance to be free... no! I smile for a chance to show the world the true me.

A chance before I expire; to go out, teach, and inspire.

Hoping that no one will longer need to wear; the mask of a pariah.

Afterthought: I dedicate to those who wear the mask. Your friends and family love and miss you. Think about the thing you do, and live the life you know is true.

The thoughts behind
Pariah mask

I wrote the pariah mask after spending four months in jail. Watching and listening day in and day out to those around me. I notice there were two sides to most of them. First, there is the side that is portrayed, in order to be accepted in the lifestyle that brought them to jail. The second was the side I call the truth side.

You don't get to see this side that often unless you're paying attention or happen to catch it accidentally. This poem was based on those I have encountered in jail, however "pariah" meaning a social outcast can be anyone; you don't have to be living the drug/gang lifestyle to put on this mask. I believe everyone wears a mask of some sort, and for a variety of reasons. It could be weight issues, drugs/alcohol, societal problems; the list goes on. Whatever the issue(s) are that makes you feel you can't be yourself, that's the reason for putting on that mask you wear.

Therefore, who or what is responsible for the mask you're wearing? Well, in the poem, I said society. I believe that's partly true, and this may come a shocker, but you, me, we are mostly responsible for the mask we wear. I bet you don't like hearing that do you? You don't want to accept the fact that we are the higher percentage reason for putting on that mask every day.

Let's look at this. Society, society says "Hey! Look, we have standards, and if you want to be a part of us, then you have to meet these standards. You have to look a certain way, act a certain way, wear this style of clothes, and participate in these activities. If you don't, then it's unacceptable, and there is something wrong with you." You are the problem. Society – AKA, peer pressure, I know you're sighing, saying, "here you go with the peer pressure angle." Your right I am, because peer pressure is a real thing, and it not only happens to children, but adults as well (peers), and it's compelling.

Only if we let ourselves succumb to this peer pressure. As humans, one of the many abilities we possess is the power to choose. I can sense another heavy sigh coming again. I know you've heard all about this power of choice, but I think it's worth another visit. I understand. You did not choose to be teased, harassed or even tormented by those who thought you didn't fit in. However, it was your choice of how you responded to it. Remember this "how people treat you is their karma; how you respond to it is yours."

For most of us, yes, I did as well. We chose to compromise on who we are to fit in. We put on the mask when we were around those we were trying to fit in with and took it off around those who accepted us for who we truly are. Not much of a compromise is it? We start to develop our character at a very young age. This character is who we indeed are. As the years' pass, we might change physically, we might even change our style of clothes or even hairstyles, but these things don't change our character, which we are on the inside.

How do we go about taking off this mask? I'm glad you asked. The first step is getting comfortable in your skin. "Heard it before Mr. Original, but what does that really mean?" To be okay with you not just some of the time, but do I dare say it be proud of who you are all of the time, despite what others might say and or do or even think of you. Let me let you in on a little epiphany I had. Everyone is so worried and thinking about what others are thinking of him or her. If that's the case, then people really don't have the time to be thinking about you, now do they? I'm just saying.

The second step in taking off the mask is to realize and accept that mask or no mask; no one is perfect. This step is so vital to do because if you don't, you'll spend your whole life trying to look perfect, that you'll end up changing the essence of who you are as a whole.

The third, last and the hardest step in taking off the mask is? I think you've guessed it right; it is taking it off. Whether it's mentally or physically taking it off will be challenging. I don't mean take it off and put it in the closet for a rainy day. I mean take it off and destroy it, may it never be worn again Then announce to the world this is (insert your name here) hear me roar.

You can't be caught up on what others call flaws. It is those flaws or how I like to put it character high lights that make us unique and ultimately makes you, you. Now that you have taken off that mask, you're going to find this new found acceptance of ones self-very rewarding. You'll attract people to you who otherwise might have thought were too good for you to be around. Your circle of influence will grow. You'll probably even hear old friends say that they didn't recognize you, not that you were wearing a physical mask all this time (or maybe you were,) but for the fact that you took off the mental one. You can only be you, so be it.

Now that you are aware that everyone wears some type of mask, I hope that you'll try to look beyond the mask and get to know people, for who he or she really is. Let them know, that for there to be you and me; our relationship, whatever it maybe has to be mask free. (That's the poet in me)

Ask yourself

1) *Do I wear a Mask?*

2) *What is it that's causing me to put on the mask?*

3) *Who is the true me?*

4) *What do I like about myself that others don't see?*

5) *What do others like about me that I don't see?*

6) *Am I ready to take the mask off for good?*

CHAPTER 2

The problem with life

The problem with life, is that it is daily,

Come on, I know deep down you agree with me.

Seven days a week, I get you think is one too many,

Now your hardest task is to choose one or two

To pretend you are free.

Monday meet controversy, Tuesday meet anxiety,

Wednesday meet worry, Thursday meet contempt,

Friday meet excitement, Saturday meet family,

Sunday meet relief.

Fifty-two weeks a year and;

You dare ask where I find serenity.

So as you attempt to live your life, raise your kids, be a good husband or a good wife, don't forget to be social.

Attend to your extended family, and your crazy friends.

When there seems to be no time left in your busy schedule, you'll still have to show you're in control.

So don't get nervous, or lose your focus, know you're not the only ringmaster of your very own circus.

We go through life trying to please this person today, and that person tomorrow.

Minding our P's and Q's watching every word we say.

Most people don't do it very effectively. While they drown, their hopes of trying climb that ladder to social and corporate hierarchy.

I use these analogies of why the problem with life is that it's daily, and I pause with a definitive thought.

Let's give this a shot.

Although life is daily, let's live it spiritually, and completely. Then and only then will we live a life that is at least semi carefree.

The Thoughts Behind
The problem with life

*Y*ou ever ask someone, how are you? Then wish you had not. Now, you are forced to listen to a barrage of complaint of how life is so unfair, why me, and a few other whoa is me's. I've come up with a solution for this when I'm asked that question. I answer, "Are you just asking, or do you want to know? Some may see this as rude. I see it as a way of allowing the person to be honest.

I compared life to a circus because it can be fun at times, while for others frightening. If you can remember the traditional circus, they performed them in a tent with one ring. Fast forward, a few decades, and it evolved into 3-ring spectacles performed in stadiums. More lights, more action, more bangs, and of course more bucks. How hard was it for you to focus on all three rings? It was frustrating at times. Was it not? You usually missed something in one or the other rings.

Today's circus's such as the big apple, cirque, has stuck to tradition one ring, under a tent keeping in mind the K.I.S.S method. (Keep it simple silly). I'm sure you're thinking "ok enough with the circus analogies, how does this relate to my life"?

As you read a problem with life, did it strike an accord with you? Are you the ringmaster of your circus? Does your life have more than two to three rings? If you answered yes to any of those questions. Congratulations, you have been diagnosed as a control freak. Yes! I went there. If you don't think so, then delegate a ring or two to someone else. Upon hearing that I bet right away, your mind was shooting on all cylinders.

Thinking of why you couldn't delegate. How you do this or that just the right way. You probably believe that old cliché, "if you want something done right, you have to do it yourself." Let me ask you this. With whom does that show more incompetence? Think about that for a minute. I'll throw a few more cliché's at you that I've either used or heard used a thousand times, such as: "life is what you make of it." There's a lot of truth to that, but it shouldn't stop there. There is that famous quote from the movie Forrest Gump? Where Forrest declares, "life is like a box of chocolates, you never know what you're going to get."

How true it is, I don't know about you, but my box never seems to have enough of my favorite kinds, then I'm left with ones I'm not that fond of. What if you're the lucky one who happens to get a box of all your favorite flavors, you notice how quickly your favorite becomes everyone else's favorite. Before you know it the box is, empty and you've only eaten a couple, so to say life is like a box of chocolates would be saying that everything about life is sweet, silky smooth and delicious and we all know that's not always the case.

As a magician, this one is my favorite. "you have to play with the hand life dealt you." Let's equate that to some card games for the sake of it. You have the ever-popular poker, no poker is good for those who like to gamble, and we all know what risks you take in gambling, most of the time you are on the losing end. Some would say that life its self is a gamble. What do you think? Are you living life like playing a poker game, are you all in?

Sometimes life can feel like war and like in any war is there really a winner? How about the classic game Go! Fish, now there is a life game. You ask for something if others do not have it, you fish until you get. The rule doesn't state that you take it from others.

My all-time favorite card game was the match game (memory). Find the compatible match. The key to this game is to remember not only the cards you reveal but also what your opponents reveal. What I'm getting at is your not just playing with the cards your dealt; you maneuver and strategize until you get something you can work with.

At the end of the poem, I suggest that we live spiritually and completely. How does one actually do that? I can only tell you what worked for me. It was not until I re-established my relationship with Christ, that I was able to see a reduction in my whining, worrying, and constant working. Now I know you're thinking. "The first two okay I can see that, but working?" You "have to work to live." Bingo! You just said it, work to live. That is how life is supposed to be. However these days many, people live to work, and for what, usually to make more money to buy more stuff, to get into more dept? The cycle is never-ending, and once you enter that, cycle you're not doing much living.

I was one of those who lived to work; this was my way to escape, to keep my mind on anything other than the things that were causing me to want to put on that mask we talked about earlier. Little did I know that my job and working all the time was actually my mask. "OK I get it, but what about this living completely"? You're asking.

Think about your life. Do you or have you ever felt like something is missing? What are those things, or people who are missing from your life, that if you had those things or people in it life would seem well complete? I am happy to tell you that I've found those things for myself and the title of this book says it all. I needed to live, love, and laugh more.

I can attest that there is more to life than.... You fill in the blank. You can't just be sitting around waiting for someone to tell you what it is. All you have to do to figure it out is to start living.

Ask yourself

1) *Who or what am I living for?*

2) *What are some of the problems with the life I'm dealing with?*

3) *Am I willing to drop or delegate some responsibilities?*

4) *Could I live without certain things? If not, why?*

CHAPTER 3

When I'm Alone

I think about the times; you know my first time, the last time, and that one time. I think about the world abroad, and all the places I'd like to see. Think I think about all the horrible things traveling could bring to me.

When I'm alone, I think,

I think about when I was young and asked; that age-old question. "What would you like to be when you grow up"? Alive was my answer without any hesitation.

When I'm alone, I think it's my mind,

I think about what the future will be, hoping there will be one for me. I think about the oddest of things like; the vastness of space, or how fast technology is growing, changing the human race.

When I'm stressed or get overwhelmed, I think of driving down a country road, or sailing the open seas, anything for a change of pace.

When I'm alone, I think it's my mind. Do you mind?

I think about God in the heavens above. I think about his grace and unfailing love. I think about what will happen when I die, remembering God's promise, believe in him, and I will never.

A life with no reasons to cry, and as I think about that, and all I can do is sigh.

When I'm alone I think, now if you don't mind; hmm.

The thoughts behind
When I'm alone

*T*his one was fun to write. It was my first, written many years ago when I visited one of my mentee's school. surprisingly enough they just happened to be discussing and writing poems. The original version of this poem was only seven lines, but as you can see I've thought some more and expanded it to the poem you've just read.

You overthink. Have ever been accused of that. Hogwash I Believe there is no such thing as overthinking. The world would not be as advanced as it is if people didn't always think. However, on the other side, it can also be said that the world wouldn't be in shape; it's in if they thought about the consequences of these advancements. In this case people are accused of not thing it through.

As I think of my thoughts as a child versus my thoughts today, I've realized they're not that different. Yes, they're more in-depth, and have more clarity to them, but overall still the same. After all, there are only3 phases of thought. There are the past, present, and future to think about. Like when I was a kid, I somehow managed to go through all 3 phases in a single moment. I really had an active imagination that caused me to think of the craziest things. I can remember the countless times my teacher would ask, "Are you with us, Eric?" Even though I was in a classroom full of students; and yet; I still was alone and guess what I was doing? You got it I was deep in thought.

I said earlier that my thoughts haven't changed since I was a kid, and they haven't. When I was a kid, I thought about death and heaven. Why was that? That's a story for another time, but ever since I re-dedicated my life to Christ, I'm finding myself thinking more and more of what it would be like in heaven. I'm not looking to die anytime soon. It's like when you're planning a vacation; you start to think about it for months, sometimes even years before you go, well, magnify that times a thousand.

I can honestly say that I have not once thought about my life issues such as; rent, work, or lack of, relationships. Most of these situations, people view as a challenge. That being said, I do think of possible solutions to other people's issues. I don't dare share them. Don't ask me why? I'm not entirely sure of the answer to that, and perhaps I feel it's better to leave it to their faith, that God is in control.

When I say I'm alone, I'm talking about mentally mostly, but sometimes physically. Are there times when I feel emotionally alone? Yes, or I should say that I used to. Those were unfortunate times in my life. It's been years since I've felt that way, and I don't think I'll feel that that way ever again. You see although I may be physically, mentally, and emotionally alone, however as a Christian I don't think I should never feel spiritually alone and that pretty much voids all the other ways to feel alone. The fact of the matter is that with God, I'm never truly alone, am I? For those who think they're better off alone, I have something to say about that, but you'll read about that in another chapter.

Ask yourself

1) *Have I given any thought of what I think about when I'm alone whether it's physically, mentally, emotionally, or spiritually? If not, start doing so.*

2) *Are those thoughts negative, positive?*

3) *Do I feel alone even with a house full of people, or at school, maybe at work?*

4) *Have I expressed those feelings and thoughts to anyone?*

5) *The next time you're "alone," thinking, write those thoughts down.*

CHAPTER 4

Orion's song

Orion's song does not come from a Grammy winner or the top 100 charts. The songs I hear sometimes tug at my heart or simply puts me in deep thought.

Ssh! Stop! Do you hear it? What? "That sound." Where? "I don't hear a thing." Well, I not only listen to it, but I also claim it, embrace it, and feel it.

I see the trees sway back and forth with a bend. I wonder what's the cause, and I listened to no end until the answer hits me; their songs relate to the wind.

This causes me to listen for natures other dialogs. The chirps of birds, drops of rain, sounds of humans, even the barking of dogs, All are nature's songs, telling me they belong.

As I listen, my heartbeats, foot taps, head nods, then I smile. I don't resist because resistance is futile.

Afterthought: Quoting; the great Sachamo, "What a wonderful world." God has created. Take time to enjoy it.

Thoughts behind
Orion's song

I love music, but if read Orion's Song and thought, "what's this got to do with music? Then you missed the point. Even as a young child, I have always been in tuned to the sounds around me. It wasn't until much later in life on a couple of occasions that I was made aware of how in tune I was.

The first time was somewhat of self-awareness. It happened while watching the movie "august rush" if you haven't seen it I recommend you rent, Netflix it, just go see it. I will not discuss details of the movie, but one of the remarkable things is there's a musical prodigy who is about 11-12 years of age, he runs away from the orphanage ends up homeless in NY City. He ends up attending Julliard. "You'll have to watch the movie to find out how that happens. Eventually, He ends up playing this huge concert in central park his very own composed piece. "I thought you said this has nothing to do with music." Give me a second. Here's where I related to the move or at least august. The piece he composed came from the sounds he heard around him while he traversed NY City. He took sounds such as bouncing of balls, the whoosh of revolving doors, even the honking of car horns. All the sounds we hear every day that we either ignore or complain about. This kid wrote a great piece of classical music. All it took was his awareness of the sounds around him. Yes, I realize it's just a movie, but the message was; clear at least to me.

In 2009, on a second occasion, something was brought to my attention. While I was riding home from work on my Segway one evening, and it was around 6 pm in the summer, so it was still light out. I usually take the same route home by way of the bike path. This particular evening, I was close to home, and I noticed and heard this person beeping his horn and waving at me. I got off the bike path and rode to the curb to where he was pulled over. He began to explain to me that for the past 2 wks

we have been riding parallel to one another, every day around this time. Coincidence I think not, mind you he is in a car and I'm on a Segway that only goes 12 mph max. Need I say more? This person says that he notices me only because of how happy and serene I looked, always smiling while riding that thing (meaning the Segway). He then asked me what I was listening to while riding. I told him none, he seemed surprised at this, I explained to him how the sounds around me make me feel so alive, and that's what puts me in the state he sees me in.

He goes on to tell me how seeing me every day has affected his mood while driving in traffic on the way home. He's found himself getting home in a brighter mood, so much so that his wife and kids have taken notice.

"What are you getting at? Have you heard the saying wake up and smell the coffee? Well, I'm saying wake up and hear the world. Many people are almost aware of the sounds of the world. These people own ambient sound machines. The downfall to those is that they're used to put you to sleep. Wouldn't it be just as relaxing to hear those same sounds while you're awake and living life?

I guess the point I'm driving home is that. God has created this amazing planet and everything on it, would it hurt you that much to take some time out of your busy life and acknowledge it?

I don't mean for you to become a tree hugger or anything of that sort. All I'm saying is hey! The next time it snows, instead of complaining about having to shovel it, or the traffic it causes, or whatever gripe you may have, think about how in two feet of snow there are no two snowflakes alike.

To those who live in hotter regions; stop complaining about how hot it is. Take some time to marvel at the fact of how hot the surface of the sun is yet our planet is positioned just right to keep us from getting any more heated than we can stand. To know that if we were any closer, we would burn to death, or if we were any, further away we would freeze to death.

Kindly Stop and take a deep breath, and as you let it out listen to the sounds around you. It's funny how you can take people from the city and put them out in the countryside, and minutes after being there, they will start complaining about how quiet it is. At night, they can't seem to fall asleep. Do you know why? Because of the sound of silence (thank you, Simon and Garfunkel)

Now reverse the situation, take people from the countryside to the city, and yet again minutes after being there, they too will start to complain of how it's too noisy. "How do people live here"? They question with disgust. They need their peace, the calm and serenity. This proves that people are somewhat aware of the sounds around them or the lack of it. I bring this to light with hopes to get people to stop and purposely take in the sounds a few minutes a day, and maybe just maybe you will find your song.

Ask yourself

1) *Is there a natural sound that you've noticed, and it tends to make you smile?*

2) *When was the last time I stopped and smelled the proverbial roses, or listened to a rainstorm?*

3) *What would it take to get me to spend some time with nature?*

CHAPTER 5

All by yourself

To think you can achieve anything all by yourself. It is such a bold and significant statement. For anyone to think, let alone say aloud, but not for a small-minded person.

For you to think of just yourself, you're only inviting whatever situation to worsen.

I have to be self-sufficient, self- reliant, and self-motivated you exclaim. Well if that's true then why is your state of affairs still the same?

You can do bad by yourself, you say. Well, with that attitude by yourself is where you'll stay. Created to achieve we were, to be great. That's how God has planned your fate, not in solitude, but together in multitudes.

In my opinion, the word self is often overstated, with billions of people in the world, I would say self is overrated

Here's a thought, while you're eating a huge helping from your self —dish, next to the peas, greens, go ahead and add a double serving of that self-fish.

Once you're nice and full and ready for nap, get yourself some coffee so you'll be nice and alert, because I'm serving inter-dependant pie for dessert.

Thoughts behind
All by yourself

I wrote this poem as a response to a conversation with a friend named Smokey. For some personal reason, he was all done with the human race. He had written us all off. There is no room on this planet for him and the other billions, so let get rid of the billions. I mean he was like "I'm going to focus on me, me, and me." Everything was about me, he sounded like he was warming up for the opera (me, me, me, meeee). After 15 minutes, with a few's, unh hum's, and is that so from me, I walked away feeling a bit down.

I wasn't sure how to respond to Smokey. That night I wrote this poem. The next day I handed it to him, as he read it, I could see him turning crimson. I wasn't quite sure what was causing it. I just had to wait until he finished reading it. When he did finish he looked at me and asked, "Was I that bad?" Actually you were worse I replied.

Smokey began to explain his frustration with people; and how people always let him down, how he does what he can for others, yet when he needs help, there is none. We had another talk this time he listened. Maybe you know of people with that attitude, or perhaps you heard a bit of yourself in

Smokey's ranting. If so, it's ok in a sense, because I know you don't mean it. You will realize this once you've calmed down and hear how ridiculous it sounds.

I want you to pick any city or town in the world; now imagine that you are the only one who lives there. Now imagine you being the only person in the world. Do you want that? I didn't think so.

There was a person who was the only person on earth, maybe you've heard of him. His name is Adam, now even though there were all sorts of animals; Adam was the first human being at one time. This didn't last too long; it might have been a day or two who knows. God realized that man was not to be alone, and he created eve, his partner and wife. I think it's safe to say that the saying "me, myself, and I became irrelevant many centuries ago.

let's face the facts, we're human, so weshould expect to be disappointed, forgotten, left out, mistreated, and a whole bunch of other things that will leave us feeling we are better off alone (yes I know that's a song)

I challenge you to write down five, no two things you can accomplish all by yourself, and I mean absolutely all by yourself. I've tried, and I can't come up with even one. How did you do? Most people think about dependency as either being a dependant or independent I believe it goes one step further and these are just my belief. According to where you live in the world, most governments consider the dependency stage from birth to about the age of eighteen. However, for some that stage is a bit long, while for some it's too long.

Why are we in such a hurry to get to that coveted independent stage? Where we now believe we are on our own, can do what we want, don't have to listen to anyone, and we can do what we want, we can make our own rules. How long did that last for you? Before you started to miss; 'the good old days".

I believe there is one more stage; it's the co-dependency or what I also call the interdependency stage. "What is interdependency stage all about"? You ask. It's like being in business for yourself, but not by yourself. It's being independent while helping, teaching and supporting each other. In doing so more people can reach some level of success no matter what that means to each individual. For some this may sound drab, but the good news is (not that good news) we get to decide whom those people are we are going to be interdependent. (While we think we are choosing) that could be bad news for some, especially if they're picking the wrong people.

Many years ago, I heard a great quote. I don't remember who said it now, but it goes something like this. "You are the average of the five people you hang around". If you are scratching your head in bewilderment, join the club. I've thought about that quote for days after hearing it. I even tried calculating it, to figure out how to get myself on the positive side of the five. I seriously had on paper what looked like some complex algorithm trying not to be average. Besides, I'm not that good with math.

Then I decided to email the speaker whoever he was, and ask him how do I go about not being average? He said to me that I have to get around people who I aspire to be like, who were in life where I wanted to be. He said, "it's straightforward, if you want to be a carpenter hang around a bunch of carpenters. If you want to be a teacher, make sure you finish your schooling". Then he simplified it. "Whatever you want to be or do in life, get around those who are there or heading there. Ask questions, but mostly listen, take notes, learn as much as you can and then copy it. This is interdependent. Now you get it.

Ask yourself

1) *Have I been trying to go at life alone?*

2) *Do I know where I want to be in life?*

3) *Are my dreams for the future something I have decided I have to do on my own?*

4) *Do I expect handouts or a hand up?*

5) *Have I been picking the wrong co-dependents*

6) *Am I the average of the five friends do I hang around? Who are the five people?*

CHAPTER 6

Hear me!

I speak, and as your listening, I can see that understanding is
missing. It seems to me like I'm speaking in code. When in
truth what I'm saying is nothing new, but many years old.

It seems to me that what I say to you in undecipherable. Hear
me; you'll see what I'm saying is actually recognizable.

I turn to my friends and family, hoping to share some personal
information, but I can tell from the expressions on their faces
that frustration and anger are now in place.

I come to you with heartache and pain, but all I get in return is
your finger-pointing and blame. I feel bad enough without
having to deal with your condescending shame.

I really need you to hear me, without your sympathy or
judgmental advice, when it's your focus and your attention will
more than suffice.

Not being listened to only adds to my frustrations, but me
being heard will release me from this ongoing suffocation, so

to help me gain some tranquility; I do not need you to listen to me. I need you to hear me!

Afterthought: you have two ears and one mouth. Learn to use them in that proportion.

Thoughts behind
Hear me!

I have always been that person people came to when they needed someone to talk with. So much so, that I could be taking the local train somewhere, and by the time I get to my stop I know much more than I should about the life of a person who was just minutes ago was a perfect stranger. Who felt that I was someone, whom they felt comfortable enough with me to share their thoughts. Someone who would not only listen to them but hear them.

Is there a difference between listening and hearing? Most people would say no. Their thoughts are "if I'm listening, then I'm hearing." What do you think? Maybe this will help you to decide.

Imagine that you were a child. You are in your room watching TV, or playing with your toys. One of your parents comes in and says:

Parent: "I want you to put away your clothes, and clean up your room."

Child: still playing or watching, says, "unh, huh."

Parent: "Are you listening"?

Child: "yeah, I'm listening,."

Parent: "then what did I say"?

Child: "you said something about my clothes."

Parent: "put that down and turn that off so you can hear me."

Sounds familiar? Now do you think there is a difference? I believe it is important to know the difference, especially if you're lucky enough to be someone's confidant. They will expect you to hear what they have to say. To the parents this is even more so for you. Why is this? Well knowing the difference will set the tone for your relationship with your children. For them knowing whether they feel they are being heard when they come to you, will establish trust, confidence, and empowerment in your child (ren). Hearing them will require some extra effort on your part, but believe me the benefits will outweigh that extra effort. Many times hearing will lead to an advance warning to a potentially life-altering situation. The hearing will sometimes give you the answers to ongoing mischief your child may be getting into. As I said in the poems afterthought, there is a reason we have two ears and one mouth. How do you know if you're just a listener or a hearer?

1) do you drop what you're doing, or set time aside when you can give your undivided attention?

2) are you in a rush to give advice they didn't ask for, or might not want just yet?

3) do you make jokes or downplay their issues?

4) Are you feeling the emotions they're emitting? (This doesn't mean you have to get all emotional, just acknowledge theirs)

5) do they come back to you often?

If you answered yes to questions 1, 3, 5 then you most like are a hearer, but if you said yes to 2, 4 then you have some work to do.

"What do I do with the info being shared"? Do nothing just yet. Do allot of hearing. Most of the times when people come to talk to us, we tend to take that as a sign that we are to fix their situations, and many times that's just not the case. Instead, wait until you hear these words; what do you think? What would you do? Can you give me some advice? Only when you're asked should your advice be offered.

Remember advice is just that. It's not always the right answer, we'd like to think we have all the answers, but we know we don't. There's only one is God. This is my mantra on advice "if you know the difference between good advice and bad advice, then you don't need any advice. With that being said, wouldn't the best advice be to tell them to pray about it or pray with them?

Not everyone has this gift of hearing, if you're not one don't beat yourself up over it, maybe you know; in fact, I know you know someone who does have it. Probably someone you go to all the time. Perhaps it's the other parent, a friend of the family, another family member, a teacher, or a cleric. Whoever it may be, recommend them. Many times, you will not even have to; they'll just naturally gravitate to that person, the same way you were drawn to your confidant.

The important thing is that the people who trust you enough to bring you their concerns feels that they are truly being heard and that a respectable person is doing the hearing. I've given you some "ask yourself" questions already, but here's a few more.

Ask yourself

1) *Am I a person that I would bring my issues to?*

2) *Do people constantly come to you to talk? Why And or why not? Really, explore this question.*

3) *Am I a gossiper?*

4) *How much am I ready to handle from other? Based on these and the questions earlier you should be able to tell whether you are a hearer or just a listener.*

CHAPTER 7

Today and tomorrow

You can't live for tomorrow while your living for today. Why?
Because it's just not meant to work that way.

Today is not here to stay, in twenty-four hours; it's going to
wither away. More hours you cannot borrow for those hours
belong to tomorrow.

Tomorrow is the future for however close it may be. Today is
the here and now, but most of all today is momentary.

Don't put off today, to wait for tomorrow, for tomorrow may
never come. Oh! We can plan for it, and get all excited, but do
remember tomorrow is not guaranteed to anyone.

I don't care what little orphan Annie said, there's not always a
tomorrow, even if it is only a day away. It's a comforting
thought for tomorrow is consistently sought.

So live for today, go out and play. Make sure to tell your loved
ones all those things you would like to say.

Before the end of that beautiful day, you might want to pray,

that tomorrow will become your new today.

Thought behind
Today and tomorrow

*A*n acquaintance of mine by name of c. Leone; inspired this poem. One day she was telling me how she had so much to do when she got off work. The next day when I saw her I ask. How much work did you get done? She looked away from me as if embarrassed, then said that she got nothing done because she was so over whelmed by all that needed to be done.

She admitted that she had an issue with not being able to focus on the task or even one day at a time.

I would bet that a good percentage of us have this exact same issue. Some of us have the nerve to say that we're "multi-tasking". Give me a break you and I both know that's not what you're doing. We have to be honest with ourselves to realize it.

We live in such a competitive society, that we feel that if we can't stay ahead of the curve, we will lose out. In all actuality by not focusing on the moment, the here and now, you are truly missing out.

I'm not saying it's wrong to plan, planning is good. It gives most people a sense of accomplishment, organization, and is a calming effect for them. Moreover, for those of you who like to procrastinate? I don't think there is such thing personally; I just think that whatever it is you're putting off doing just isn't important enough for you.

Are you one of those peoples who are famous for saying things such as; "I'll get it done tomorrow"; "I have plenty of time to get it done?" My favorite, "I work well under pressure. Then all of a sudden, the tomorrows turn into weeks, plenty of time, turns into running out of time, and the pressure turns into stress.

If you're like this as an adult, I bet you were probably the same as a child. Remember when you were in school and you got an assignment, how many times did you wait until the night before you even started it? You may very well work well under pressure, but I bet your family, friends, and co – workers do not.

We've all heard the saying: "we all have 24 hours in a day; it's what you do with it that counts". My question to you is why are so many people trying to squeeze 168 hours, a week's worth into those 24 hours while others are trying to turn 24 hours into 168 hours? Only you can answer that, but I'm going to go out on a limb and suggest that there's a lack of sense of time in play, so here's a breakdown of a day.

1 day = 24 hours

24 hours = 1,440 minutes

1,440 minutes = 80,400 seconds

How many of those seconds did it just take you to read that? Maybe 4 to 5? In addition, you still have plenty left to do whatever. I hope a light bulb just went off for you.

For those of you who tend to take things to the extreme, I'm not suggesting for you to plan your day to the second, that will only cause more stress than it's worth, however if we planned our days with a bit more detail, we'll find there's so much more you can get done in it .

You'll find there is time to work, to play, to give to the kids, to spend with your spouse, and most importantly time to spend on yourself, that illustrious "me time". Don't let your day end with regrets that you didn't take the time to do those things you felt in your heart you should have done.

"Here today gone tomorrow" you've heard this quote before I assume. Nevertheless, have you experienced it? Like a job or a loved one like a parent, child, friend, maybe your own health. I've experienced the loss of all the above here one day, gone the next, and with that lost came the regret. Regret that I took time to plan for a future with them all; everything was "one day

I'll…, but I couldn't… I mean I didn't find the time or I didn't make the time to give them my today.

today is what really matters. Because it's here and now, and with today, you have some control of how you deal with it. Yesterday is gone, what's done is done, tomorrow has yet to arrive, and who know if it will.

Time is money

We have all heard this phrase "time is money" there is some truth to that, at least in the sense of value. Many people have jobs where they trade their time for dollars, but there are people who also value their time as much as if it was money, and if they are anything like me, I loathe wasting time. If you and I made plans to go out and I was to pick you up at a predetermined time and you are not ready, I just leave, I feel like you don't value my time.

Unlike money, time once spent you can't get it back; there's no refunds, or credit. Its value doesn't fluctuate like money. I believe my time is priceless, and I would hope many others do as well. Those who don't aren't doing much with the time they have.

There are books in the bible that talks about time, but my favorite is in Ecclesiastes, chapter 3. The first verse reads; for everything, there is a season, and time for matter under heaven. ("So that's where the Byrds got that from")

Then in verse 2-8 it goes on to list things in life that there is time for. You may read it and ask. "Can I really do all that in 24 hours?" My answer to that would b an honest yes, are we expected to have all those experiences in one day? That would be a strong no, but we never know, could happen.

I think to sum it up Gods warning us that we don't know when our time will be up on this earth, so experience all the wonders of life while we can. So that when you're asked, "what did you do today"? You get all excited to tell.

Ask yourself

1) *Do I manage my time well?*

2) *How do I value other and my time?*

3) *How can I make the most of my time?*

4) *How can I fill my today to make it harder to be better tomorrow? Then repeat.*

CHAPTER 8

The stranger

My friends and family have given up on me, but you a stranger have come to embrace me.

For all the times I wanted to run and hide, you a stranger who was always by my side.

You are there to comfort me when I feel down, you give me strength when I feel weak, love me when no one else would. All this from a stranger, I've never understood.

When I needed a shoulder to lean on somehow, yours was always around, when no others could be found. No matter the time day or night, you are always there to be my guiding light.

I often wonder you a stranger, how can this be. then I realized the irony, that the true stranger was me.

The thoughts behind
The stranger

So often, I hear the phrase "I found God when…then I thought about how paradoxical this phrase is. In order to find something would it not have to be lost first? If that is the case, why is it that people always see God as the lost entity? Wouldn't you find it ridiculous, that the creator of everything being lost?

"So your saying Gods isn't lost, does that then mean I'm the one lost?" I do not see that as the case either. God knows everyone of us, and everything about us even where we are physically, mentally, and emotionally at any given point.

"If Gods not lost and we are not lost to him, then how is it that we get separated from him? The quick and easy answer is we sin, but I will elaborate on it. God has given us freedom of choice, and with that freedom, we chose to ignore god and his teachings, guidance. Once we make that choice to become estranged sort of speaking from God. Hence, the reason I chose this title for the poem.

The poem started with my mindset on god being the stranger. I was all ready to point my fingers and rant you! you! You! then something wonderful happened. While listening to a program on a Christian radio station, I heard a message. The message was so profound I could have sworn the speaker was in the same room talking directly to me.

Here is what the message was. The speaker was explaining a scene in the movie "hook" starring Robin Williams. He said his favorite scene in the movie was when the now grown up peter pan makes his way back to Neverland. Once there he sets out to find the lost boys. (how ironic right?)

He finds them only, he is not welcomed with open arms, and in fact, they attacked him. As peter pleaded to his once friends, that he was indeed peter pan just grown up, a lost boy who happens to be blind walks over to pan, puts his hands on pans face and begins to contort his facial muscles into different expressions till he found one he recognized, a smiling happy peter. Then he exclaimed, "there you are peter".

The host of the radio show said some other things, but I couldn't even begin to tell you what they were. I heard all I needed, and some might even say all I was suppose to hear. I immediately tore up the original version of the poem, kept the title and wrote the poem you've just read.

I knew of Christ, his love and his forgiveness, but I refused to let him into my life but not for long. I didn't want God to have totally control of my life. (oops getting a little ahead of myself)

I was reluctant, but as I looked back on my life; now I can clearly see where God has stepped in and gave me a stern no! Not yet! or as written in the poem He has given me comfort, love, and strength. Whatever I needed to weather the storms I've faced. So if God has always been with me. It only makes sense I would be the stranger.

Have you ever had a friend you've known for many years, but over the years, things got distant? They had kids, you moved away, but they kept in touch. I say "they" for a reason. Although you both had each other's phone numbers, addresses, and emails, they were the ones who did the reaching out.

Then one day you all decide to get together and hang out. When the day finally comes and you people are finally together, the first thing out of your mouth is "hey stranger". See what I'm getting at? That is what we as strangers say to those we have avoided for whatever reason.

That's what I was originally going to accuse God of being. Reality then slapped me in the face, and I could see how much of a stranger I was to God, and then I decided to have a relationship with him. I confess I probably would not have come to that decision if it were not for God laying his hands on me, stripping away at the layers of shame, guilt, anger, unforgiveness, and whatever other negative things my soul was harboring. God just kept stripping away until he was able to say, "There you are my child".

There are many verses in the bible that re- enforces Gods promises, that he will never leave and or abandon us. I don't know about you, but that gives me comfort. It's a comfort to know that even though our friends and family may turn their backs on us you can always count on god to be with you.

If you find that you're a stranger to God, I urge you to get to know him for yourself. You'll be glad you did. God is looking forward to peeling away your layers and saying "here you are my child".

Ask yourself

1) *Have I given any thought to my relationship with god?*

2) *Do I really want one?*

3) *Am I ready to accept Jesus as my lord and savior?*

If you said yes to any of those questions, then pray this prayer aloud, it shouldn't matter who's around this is between you and the lord.

Father I confess that I sinned and done wrong. I believe that your son Jesus Christ took the punishment that I deserved by dying on the cross-and I thank you. I also believe that you raised him from the dead. I now receive Jesus as my personal savior and lord. Amen.

Now if you've just prayed that prayer and meant it from the heart, you are a new person in Christ. Go and seek out a Christ teaching church. We welcome to the family.

CHAPTER 9

Beneath the skin

Beneath the skin, you don't know me, but you still judge me. You say you know my kind. That makes us all the same in your mind.

beneath the skin, I breathe in air, the same air you just happen to share. He same air in which all our lugs fed. How easily we forget, cut you or cut me we all bleed red.

Beneath the skin, you and I may be kin. Which makes the line between races very thin. If history is right that means we truly are all brothers and sisters in Gods sight.

Beneath the skin we must realize, that we are all human beings, no matter the color of our skin. So to hate one another because of a color, only causes wounds, that aren't easy to mend.

The thoughts behind
Beneath the skin

I wrote this poem during a dark time in our nation, as well as dark times in nations abroad. (One of many) a time of wars, religious conflicts, but in particular the recent rash of police shootings that has caused such racial tension in many cities across the US. Even in cities where there were no incidents. Sparking an us against them attitude all over again. Not that it had truly dissipated in the first place.

I thought we were past this. I guess I thought wrong. What do they call it, wishful thinking?

Discussions on racism have always been a touchy subject to say the least. There are those who think racism no longer exists, and there are those of us who know firsthand that it does.

As a person who grew up in the 70's when racism was in your face every day, and at a time when bussing was just beginning and drew a mutual hatred in the city of Boston. I can honestly say that we have made some progress, but we are evidently not there yet, and what I mean by yet; I mean a place of acceptance, understanding, and lack of fear.

For me being a black male brought on a completely new set of challenges. Brought up to be an articulate, cultured, and open minded. I also listened to classical music, and loved theatre. I was not your typical 11-year-old kid living in an urban neighborhood. That being said, I not only had to deal with racism in general, because no matter what I listened to, how I spoke I couldn't change the fact that I was a dark skinned black boy, not that I wanted to change it. If that wasn't enough, I also had to deal with same race racism. "what"? You may be saying. Yes! It too exists, and because of my persona, I wasn't exactly "popular" with the other blacks in my neighborhood.

They assumed I was trying to be white, therefore I warranted me being called an uncle tom, or turn coat. I was fortunate enough too been placed with Christian foster parents, who really helped me by constantly encouraging me to just be me. To be honest I didn't see any other choice.

I was also lucky enough to live on one of the few streets in my neighborhood of Roxbury that was had a mix of races. Those of us kids who lived there really didn't understand all the hoopla. Well I did. We were just kids who enjoyed playing games, eating junk food, and getting wet via the fire hydrant.

I believe racism comes from fear and the fear stems from lack of understanding on all sides. I also believe that until we all make a conscience decision to attempt to get to know each other's cultures and social differences; until then; no real progress can be made to end racism.

I think if we can learn about each other's cultural differences, which I believe more and more each day are becoming less different. We can then start the healing process, and be one race, the human race.

Here's what really baffles me, you can go to any social even i.e.: concert, pro/college sport, or even an amusement park and you'll see throngs of people, all different races and cultures enjoying the same activities, slapping high fives when their team scores, or singing together along with their favorite artist who's on stage. Then at the end of the event, it's as if someone flicked a switch.

I have worked in an arena for thirteen years, and I have seen this personally at these events and except for the team, colors and the opposing team fans, everyone is colorblind. So what changes once people leave these events? What is it that causes those blinders to fall off? In addition, color now becomes an issue once again. I do not know, but we need to be asking those questions.

I use the term beneath the skin for one reason and one reason only. That reason is that I truly believe that beneath the skin we are the same. Okay, there is no exception; gender, but if we didn't have those differences would you be able to tell what race a person is, if there was no skin? Most people would answer no, and the few that would say yes, I would bet they work in the medical field of some sort. Why let a color controls your emotions. This is just one more question that we need to be asking.

As a Christian, I believe that God has made us all in his image, and that we are all unique in our own special ways. Even those who may not walk in faith believes the same. I also believe that showing hatred toward someone who is a certain color, class, ethnicity, is in essence saying that god has made a mistake. I hope we realize that, that is just not possible.

In part of the verse, most people know by heart and quote often is John 3:16 it declares "that God so loved the world..." that means everyone, there are no exceptions included in that verse. In fact, the one separation I constantly see written in the bible is the saved and unsaved, and there are going to be people of all types wherever you end up. Therefore, you are stuck sort to speak with people of all backgrounds.

Jesus gave us a new command, that we love our neighbors. He was not just talking about those people within the four blocks of your neighborhood; Jesus was talking about those people in the four directions of the compass. He also did not include any if's ands or buts'. So I ask you now, what is your excuse? No! Stop! Your answer should just be nothing.

Ask yourself

1) *Why do I you think racism exists?*

2) *Do I hold any ill will toward another race or ethnic group?*

3) *If so; why? (Remember because is and never will be an answer)*

4) *Would I be okay with having an open discussion about racism with people of other races?*

5) *If not then why? If so, why have I not already?*

CHAPTER 10

Laugh more

You; are hereby charged with lack of laughter, and when this trial is over, I will sentence you after.

How do you plea? "not guilty; your honor". "You see there's nothing about life I find funny.

Witnesses have testified that five out of seven days all you do is cry. As a defense, you argue that is it's all that helps you to get by.

Prosecutor has presented evidence, that at a party you refused not only to laugh, but to even grin."Objection" says the defense. "why should my client have to join in?

Experts have advised that laughing is infectious, which should be explored more. To that advice, your client ignored.

Prosecutors closing argument is as follows: that for the sick and the healing and for creating good feelings laughter is best. With that the prosecutor rests.

the jury walks through the door, with verdict in hand. The judge asked all to stand, while the verdict was read. Guilty as charged! and all you can do is, shake your head.

The sentence was quite funny. The Judge did not ordered jail time or to pay tons of money. His Honor ordered that we seriously explore ways to laugh more.

Afterthought: laugh to keep from crying.

The thought behind

Laugh more

The title "Laugh more" came about while sitting around a table playing cards (I was not betting) with a group of people. This particular person had such a streak of bad luck; he could not win a game even if he had to play by himself. After each game he lost, he would make a few choice comments, and make these weird facial expressions, which would cause me to laugh.

Forty-five minutes into his losing streak and my continual laughter, this person finally asks; "what's so funny?" I did not reply with what I would really want to, which was simply "you" because I could clearly see that my laughter was getting to him much more than his losing at cards. Therefore, I replied "your reactions". I said to him "you're taking this way to serious". To which he replied. "Well I don't like losing, and I don't like being laughed at even more". Can you guess what I did to that response? No, I did not laugh. I smiled. I guess that is the same as laughing to him because he blew a gasket. He wanted to fight me over it. I didn't respond to his outburst, I just walked away, and yes, I was still smiling.

I had some time to think about the situation, of how it could have played out. He might have swung on me. I; would have been forced to defend myself, and charges could have possibly been filed. I thought of how ridiculous it would have sounded to the judge, and what the proceeding would be like. Thus "laugh more" was born.

Some may read this and think that I angered that fellow. That I should not have laughed at him. To that, I must say again, that I was not laughing at him, I was laughing at his reactions. "what's the difference?" You may be asking. Simply put if he hadnot react to losing the way he did, I would have no reason to laugh. If I were laughing at him then it would not matter how he reacted, I would have still laughed.

Have you ever tried to hold back a laugh? It's hard to do, for me it's almost impossible, and when I try to, it actually hurts. I love to laugh and smile, and many who know me would agree that I'm always smiling and laughing. I'm the type of person who doesn't even mind being laughed at if the situation warrants it. I would like to believe that most people are just like me.

I cannot, so I will not try to explain all the scientific and medical properties of laughter, but I'm sure you've heard something about it if not Google it. Do you realize we are the only one of god's creations that has the ability to laugh? I know those cynic's are saying "hey Mr. Lol, what about the laughing hyena? Well, hyena's make a sound that sounds like laughter, but try telling it a joke and see if you get a laugh from it. "okay how about parrots?" That is like taking a tape recorder and playing it back; all they are doing is copying. "I got you now; what about chimpanzees?" Touché, but we will not go there, anyway your missing the point. I'm just trying to get you to see how special it is that our vocal cords allow us to make this joyous/ and sometimes annoying sound.

Have you noticed how contagious laughter is? It does not matter who is laughing, or what it's about. Has this ever happened to you? You hear someone laughing, and you do not even know what he or she are laughing about, but their laugh causes you to start laughing, or just smile. It is an amazing feeling, do you agree?

The other unique thing about laughter is that a different situation causes different types of laughs. There is the giggle, you know the one females are known for, they even have a way to write/text it he he! Then there is the popular lol or laugh out loud, and I dare you to try to stop that from coming out. Then there's my favorite, that gut-wrenching, eye tearing, knee-slapping laugh; ok no one really does the knee-slapping any more, but I bet if you saw it happening it would make you laugh even harder.

If you happen to be one of those people who walks around a frown on your face all the time, and don't like seeing others happy; I have this to say to you "don't take life so seriously, it's too short as it is." There is a saying that goes something like; "misery loves company" if that the case then I will pass, I would rather hang out with those hyenas and or parrots.

Here's a tip if you find it hard to get in a laugh at least once a day. Fake it, no I am serious now, fake it!, look into a mirror and let out a laugh. Even a fake laugh will release whatever chemical it is that makes one happy. Once you have a taste of that feeling, believe me you will want more of it.

Another tip is if you have kids spend more time with them, they will provide many opportunities to laugh, if you do not have kids spend time with nieces, nephews, younger cousins, you get the point. Kids do the darndest things. If that's not feasible, get a puppy or a kitten, pets also provide ample opportunities to laugh, and if that doesn't work and I'm very serious about this as well. Pray about it God says to "ask, knock, seek, and it will be given to you." So go ahead and ask God for a sense of humor or just the ability to lighten up a bit.

I will end this chapter with a joke:

There were these two guys, they were best friends, and they loved to take walks in the park with their radio and listen to their favorite sport; baseball. Then one day, while sitting on a bench in the park, one of the guys had a thought. He said to the other "I wonder if there is baseball in heaven?" His friend replied, "I don't know, but whoever dies fist must come back and tell the other. A year later while sitting on the same bench and missing his best friend who passed away he hears his name being called. It was his friend; he had come back as promised. He asked, "Well is there baseball in heaven?" To that his friend replied, "Well I have good news and bad news." The guy on the bench says, "Well give me the good news" his friend tells him there is baseball in heaven. The guy on the bench gets all excited and says, "Then what can possibly be the bad news?" His buddy sighs and says: you're pitching on Friday."

Does that get anything? Yes, no, maybe? Oh well, I tried.

Ask yourself

1) *Have I been accused of being too serious?*

2) *Do I get upset when I see people who always seem to be happy?*

3) *When was the last time I had a good laugh?*

If you took too long answering then I believe you are long overdue.

CHAPTER 11

"Love – 911"

Love can be a verb, meaning it requires action. Action in which everyone involved gains satisfaction.

Love can be a noun, meaning it's something that can be given away with hopes that the love is returned in much the same display.

Love is not meant to be turned on and off like a fountain of water. Nor, be bottled up like some selfish hoarder.

to say you love your car, house, job, even your pet, you say it easily, so why do you find it so hard to express your love for me?

Love should not set like the evening sun; love is meant to shine on everyone.

When love is found, the heart soars and will ache in pain when love is lost. When; our love is not blessed from God above, love will always come at a cost.

Is there more to love than it seems? You will find the answer to that question in first Corinthians chapter thirteen.

Afterthought: no matter how it's said, I love you, 143, I heart you with the hands, for most people can be tough, and because of that, we don't say it nearly enough.

The thoughts behind
Love – 911

Why love -911? Here are the reasons I chose this title for this poem. I believe the world is in a state of emergency and needs more love. As kids who were, we taught to call in case of emergency and for help. you were taught to call 911. Well when you dial love 911 it's not going to connect you to your local police, fire, health service department, this connection is going straight to heaven where the only one who can genuinely help us is, and that's God.

The other reason for the title is that I think we all need help understanding what love is, and what it is not. "come on everyone knows what love is, even kids." You might be saying right about now, but I beg to differ. I think most people have their idea of what love is or mean to them, but not necessarily what true love means.

Take music, for example, there are literally thousands upon thousands of songs about love, and in every one of them love takes on a different meaning. It would take a couple of books to go through them all, so I picked out just a few. Let's review them and find out what meaning love takes on in each.

We will start with "Love is a Battlefield" by Pat Benitar. Even if you have never been in the military, I'm sure you've seen war or battles on TV. or in the movies. There's fighting, killing, chaos, and more killing. Exactly where is the love?

So what's the rational thinking behind the title of this song? Is that love causes people to kill? That couldn't be further from the truth. Jealousy, anger, greed, and lust cause's people to kill, not love. I say if love is a battlefield, then please count me out.

The next song I chose is "what's love got to do with it" by Tina Turner. Now we all know that her life with her then husband Ike was a proverbial hell. Therefore, it would make sense that she and many other women who have been through what Tina has gone through would feel the way she did.

In the song, she asks, "what's love got to do with it?" Along with the question, "who needs a heart when a heart can be broken?" I have a question of my own. How can something so strong be so fragile? I hope by the end of this chapter I come close to answering it.

A lot of people love expecting something in return, when in truth it is all about you. And when you don't get back what you're expecting, you cry about a broken heart. Here is the thing, it's not your heart that's broken, and it's your pride and ego that has been shattered. Trust me when I tell you, you'll know when you have a broken heart; just ask a person who's had a heart attack, a double/triple bypass, or palpitations. So what does love have to do with it? Everything if it is the right kind of love. We'll talk about that a bit later.

Moving on to the next song I chose, which is; "I would do anything for love, but I won't do that" by meatloaf. I have to admit at one time in my life; I loved this song that's because I really didn't understand what love was or what it was all about then. Not that I have it all figured out now, but I do have a much better understanding of it.

I chose this song because I feel that many people relate to this song's meaning of what love is. This type of love comes with stipulations, rules, and conditions. Like; if you love me, then where's my ring, if you love me, then why won't you have sex with me?, I love you, now here sign this prenup, I love you, but I'm not "in" love with you, what does that mean; really? Here are a few more. I do love you, but I love this other person as well, and then you have I'll love you even more if you get me… {Fill in the blank}

All these are examples of what I call contract love, where you really should read the fine print, and when you do, you'll see it's not love at all. This chapter wouldn't be complete if I didn't reference the Beatles. The last song I chose is "all we need is love." I have to admit; they hit the nail on the head at least with the title and the lyrics almost spot on except for the part when it says it's easy, we all know that it's not easy to love everyone.

But they were on the right track with the title cause all we need is love if it's the right kind of love. "What do I mean by the right kind of love, and how do I know if it's the right kind of love? Is there more than one right kind of love? Yes and no. I say yes because there are three types of love that most are not aware of and they are:

Eros love – the kind of love a husband and wife share, or at least they are supposed to have for each other, passionate.

Philia love – which is the love you feel for a friend, neighbor, affectionately, you may even feel this type of love toward a pet.

Storge love - which is familial love, like between parents and their children?

Agape love – this is G

odly love or true love, unconditional love.

Now here is why I say no. Take brotherly love, for example, we've all had friends we love like family, then something happens, and an argument occurs, or maybe a fight happens, that tears up that relationship. "Wait a minute just because we

fight and argue, doesn't mean I don't love them anymore."
Hang on we will address that in a minute, but for now, let us
move on.

"So which love is the right on? "amorous, now that have to be
the one right. You might think so, but I have one word for you.
Can you guess it? It's divorce. Many times this type of love is
confused with lust. I remember when I was a teenager, and I
went to my mother and declared how in love I was with this
girl in my class. My mother looked at me with the most
endearing eyes and said, and I quote "honey that's not love,
you're in heat." My heart was broken, but at the time, I thought
it was love. As I stated earlier, it was not my heart that was
broken, it was my pride.

That leaves us with agape love which is the. Truest form of
love; however, it's also Godly love and as most of us know
there is only one God. "so are you saying that no one can
achieve this type of love on our own? Absolutely not, but with
the help from the master who is love I think we can come
pretty darn close. "how you ask?" I hope is your next question
and I'm glad you're asking.

I hinted to it in the poem, remember the last line? If you don't
take a look at it. First Corinthians chapter thirteen is a great
place to start learning about real love. Of course, there are

many other references to love in the bible; I recommend you seek those out as well. You will be surprised like I was to see that I had it all wrong. Although it may seem hopeless to achieve agape love, God expects us to strive for it; and who knows, miracles do happen. Oh! Sorry, no I didn't forget to address that question about brotherly love, I'm hoping I have stirred enough interest in you; that you'll go and read first Corinthians, chapter thirteen for yourself. There you will find answers. Now just in case you have not heard it lately, I love you in lord.

Ask yourself

1) *Before reading this what was your meaning of love?*

2) *After reading this, is love still what you believed it to be?*

3) *Which of the three kinds of love would you most like to receive?*

4) *Which of the three kinds of love are you willing to give out?*

CHAPTER 12

Situations inspired by deacon John O'Neal

I find myself dealing with situations day in and day out. Some I honestly don't know how they come about.

Face them you say, these situations in which my emotions get fed. Oh! No way, it is much easier to pretend everything is okay.

I call them situations and not problems because I have come to realize that problems start with me. Now that I have figured that out, I can accept that life; is not meant to be situation free.

As long as we are alive, situations will arise., the best way to deal with them, is to pray to God and give the situations to him.

Afterthought: "the only disability in life; is a bad attitude."

The thoughts behind
Situations

There is a line in the poem that says. I call them situations; and not problems; because problems start with me." That line which inspired this poem came from a very dear friend by the name of deacon John O'Neil, so deacon O'Neil I thank you.

After I heard this line, I thought about it for days. Something about that line appealed to me. Then it hit me like a coconut falling from a tree. While most would think of a problem or situation as same, I did not.

I've found out that I was very good at handling situations while not so good at handling problems, usually because the problems I faced were caused by something I did, or didn't do. I know some of you are thinking that's just a play on words and I would tend to agree with you, but if it helps me to be able to deal with it more calmly; so be it.

I want to address this whole play on words thing, some would say; "well there are good problems, and there are bad problems." As the comedian, John Pinette would put it "oh! Nay! Nay!" I only see the word problem in a negative light, not once have I heard anyone use the word problem this way: so and so I have this problem, my husband and I have been married for twenty-six years, and everything is great can you please help us?

I actually heard this one as a play on words. "Having too much money is a good problem to have." How can something good be a problem? The word situation, on the other hand, can have a bad or good meaning, as for my thought process; even bad situation to me seems temporary, relatively easily fixed, hey !no sweat, I got this. No matter how bad, the word situation makes it seem not all that bad.

Take NASA, for example. Do you think they would rather hear "Houston we have a situation," or the dreaded "Houston we have a problem"? If you answered neither your probably right. I'm just saying that for me the stress level wouldn't get as high hearing the situation over the word problem because you're not sure if it's good or bad, but you're pretty sure it's a bad thing when you hear the word problem. Your stress level shoots straight to high, don't pass go, don't collect $100.

Play on words is not anything new in today's society. Do you remember when bad became good? When fat became good looking? Ok its spelled phat, but you get my point right. How about when being sick didn't require a trip to the emergency room. The point is at a time when everyone is living stress-filled lives; any way to make it more manageable should not be frowned upon.

I look at what Jesus went through, and to see him handle it like it was just any old situation, that in its self is cause for praise. I don't think, no, I know I wouldn't be able to see that as a situation. It would have been a problem.

I would have had a problem being whipped, tormented, nailed to a cross, spat on, just totally disrespected, not Jesus he just took it like the champ he is, because he knew that the situation he was in was only temporary. He knew he would get through it, and be in a better place because of it. Jesus knew he was creating a way for the world to come to salvation. So now I don't go to the God with problem, I go to him with situations, with relief of knowing he is in control of all of them.

To help me get through some things, I choose wordplay, and you will see more of it in other poems. What is it for you? Do you have a technique for dealing with stressful moments; or no, I am not going to say it, or situations? Great if you do. Way to be proactive. (No this is not an endorsement) lol.

Ask yourself

1) *How do you typically respond to situations?*

2) *Look at what you perceive as problems; do you think it would be easier to deal with if you looked at them as just a situation?*

3) *Take any problems you had to face, and compare it to Jesus' situation; do you still feel as if you have problems?*

CHAPTER 13

Dark at noon

I try not to read the newspapers, or watch the local, national news. Because, it makes me sad and gives me the blues

A few fell good stories, and some acts of random kindness is not enough for me to dismiss all the poverty, hunger, homelessness, and most of all the violence.

Why are people killing each other in the name of their presumed turf? The darkness swarms over me like a hundred-foot surf.

As I look out my window, I see it dark at noon. There is no sun, stars, not even a moon.

Open your eyes if you dare to see any of my sentiment you too do share. The sins of the world have become an everyday affair.

Like a flash in the night so many fathers, mothers, sisters, brothers, and whole generations, all gone too soon. Now; their days to become dark at noon to.

Afterthought: whoever know the right thing to do, and fails to do it, for them, it is sin. – James 4:1

The thoughts behind
Dark at noon

I remember when I was about 4 – 5 years of age, and I still lived with my biological family. It was around the holiday season, and every year on TV they would show this holiday animated movie about this donkey who had really I mean; really long ears. Not only were they super long they were also very wide.

It would bother me, how badly this donkey got teased. For some reason this particular year it bothered me so much, I went crying to my mother and sisters;. I was expecting to be consoled, nurtured, maybe even hugged stupid me, because this was not the case.

Instead, I was told to "stop being so sensitive" by my mother, and I was called a sissy by my two eldest sisters. Being the only boy in a house of females and by not having my brother or father around, you would think they would encourage me to show my feeling. Boy did I think wrong. I began to suppress my feeling or at least showing them only when I was alone, which was most of the time.

Let us fast-forward a year or two when I was taken from my family and put into my second foster home for reasons I won't get into now that would take another whole book hint, hint. I got sent to this foster home, and right away, I felt the difference. The foster parents actually cared, and somehow I knew it would be ok for me be me, and let my feelings out, guess what? I was right in that assessment. My new caretakers encouraged me express my feelings anytime I felt the need. That; made me feel good.

I watched that cartoon again the next holiday season, the one with the donkey. I guess I always hoped it would turn out differently for the donkey, not this time. Again, I got upset went crying to my foster mother, knowing she would understand. Her response was very different from what I expected

She opened her arms wide, took me in and hugged me while I cried and sniffled telling her "how it was so unfair", I ask her "why do they have to treat him like that? and why does it make me feel this way all the time; he's just a cartoon character? Mary, my foster mother, extended her arms so she could look me in the eyes and said "sweetheart it's okay, you just feel too hard." somehow I knew exactly what she meant. It's not, but it is a sensitivity thing if you get what I'm saying.

I say this because it only gets to me when I am around others who are in deep pain. I'm not talking about oops I've fallen down and scraped my knee type of pain. I am talking about the soul hurting, heart-wrenching pain. These types of pains I tend to feel as if it were my own.

It does not matter if I know you personally, I could be walking down the street, riding the bus or the train, and be near someone who is going through that type of pain I mentioned earlier. I will just suddenly get sad, or my chest would start hurting as if someone was trying to rip my heart out of my chest.

I have never sought medical advice for this or told anyone about this because deep down I knew there was nothing anyone could do about it. I just accepted the fact that this was a part of me, this is who I am, my character highlight

What does one do when they seemingly feel the pains of the world? As I grew up, I found ways to deal with it, at least the best I knew how. I knew there was a common denominator in each way I came up with dealing with my unique gift. Each way had something to do with doing something for others. This was the start of my altruistic lifestyle.

I made a promise to myself that, wherever I went, whoever I met, I would always try to make people's lives better. Even if it was just for that minute or two, we interacted with one another. I wanted them to leave thinking "I'm glad I met him."

I began to volunteer for everything, and anything that I saw would help me on this altruistic quest. There was the boy scouts, explorers, neighborhood CDC's, the red cross; this list goes on. There were also the guardian angels, civil air patrol, and all sorts of charities, nonprofit walks, runs and bike rides.

Even while incarcerated, opportunities presented its self to me. I never knew it was God's plan for me, I didn't see it as such back then, but now that my focus is on Christ; I can see that it was his doing.

So why did I chose "dark as noon" as the title of this poem? You may be asking; probably a few days before I wrote this poem. I was hearing so much negative stuff going on in the world. I heard about wars, plane crashes, shootings, kidnappings, just awful things happening day in, and day out and all at once, I felt so much of this pain personally, like a wave crashing upon me. I ended up feeling really depressed, so I laid down, this was just about noontime, so I titled this poem dark at noon to remind me how dark it got for me that day at noon.

After writing the poem, I thought about the return of Christ and about what it says in revelations 6. I'm not going to tell those who don't know what it says; I'm hoping you'll get curious and read it for yourself. Let me warn you it may seem farfetched, so you might want to read it with someone who is living a Christ-filled life because you will have questions I know I did, but I am so looking forward to that day.

I think about the Ten Commandments, and why people make such a big deal of which Commandment they have kept. God clearly states if you violated one of them you have violated against them all.

At the end of my poems, I sometimes write an afterthought. On this one, I simply wrote a verse from the book of James. James 4:17; to be exact. There James simplifies things regarding the Ten Commandments by saying and I am paraphrasing here "if you know right from wrong, and you don't choose what's right, then you've sinned, it can't get any simpler.

Ask yourself

1) *Knowing right from wrong, how many times do I choose wrong?*

2) *Did I regret it?*

3) *Did I forgive myself?*

4) *Have I asked for forgiveness? (from the lord)*

5) *If not. What are you waiting for?*

CHAPTER 14

Control of me

Inspired by H. Vega

I have made mistakes and. Consequences; are now being paid. Three to five years to be exact. They have full control of me, and that's a fact!

From the time I get up to the time, I go to sleep. From what I eat, to the items I'm allowed to keep, they have control of me.

The person whom I share my cell could very well be a person from hell. I never know who it will be — just one more way they have control of me.

Even though this situation stinks, it gives me the time to think. About the changes, I need to make as a whole. To get back what I have given way, the essence of control.

Just because they now have control of me, know this; my heart, my mind, my spirit stays control by me.

Afterthought: "the only way to lose control is to give it away." – **E. Kennedy**

The Thoughts behind
Control of me

*M*y friend h. Vega asked me to write him a poem. "What about," I asked; Vega did not have a clue; he just really liked my writings and wanted something. After giving it, some thought he said he wanted one about his situation; which just happened to be our situation. I agreed to do one, but I didn't want to ask how he felt about being in jail cause I knew I would get a bunch of ranting, so I accomplished what I wanted by just having normal everyday conversations with him. The poem you just read was the result of my asking without asking. So my friend Vega, I thank you for inspiring this poem.

Vega's sense of no control comes from incarceration, which makes perfect sense, but how many people walking around this earth feeling as if they have lost control of their very own selves?

When people "lose" this control of themselves, who or what gains it. For some their addictions has the control, addictions to drugs, alcohol, sex, smoking,, and it doesn't have to be those extreme addictions, it could be an addiction to working, lying, TV, internet, or even sleeping. Someone can be addicted to many things; that seems to have taken control of them. These addictions have mental control of you.

Then there is the kind of control someone feels from a boss, or a coach, this kind of control is more of the physical type. Because of the control of your hours, pay, vacation time, and promotions. For coaches, they control your playing time, position, even your success.

It's not just the adults who feel they have no control over themselves. Many times children do as well especially teenagers. How many times have you heard them say this "you're not the boss of me?" Maybe they spoke to some other kid or an adult other than parents because that is how they feel. They equate their loss of control, to always being; told what to do. Would you believe some people feel they have lost control once they had a family? Lost control of their time, money, dreams, and aspirations. They believe all controlled by their families.

Then there is a loss of emotional control. This type of loss usually is in relationship; intimate or non-intimate. How does someone control another's emotion? The plain answer to that is they can't, but you must understand that emotional control doesn't stop there it includes mental and physical control as well.

To take emotional control of someone they first have to grind your mind down to make you believe that you are worthless; you need them to be someone or something. They give you a false sense of love and safety. You just read about love. Therefore, you now know what type of love you or someone you know may be dealing with.

I said in the afterthought of the poem that the only way to lose control is to give it away. I know many people will disagree with that, and that's ok. These are my opinions but think of the reason you or someone you may know have lost control of themselves. It could be because of the aforementioned or something I have not. What happened just before the loss of said control? You or they just gave up and gave in am I right?

Some readers might be saying to themselves or aloud. Yes, I do more than you can imagine. It happens to the best of us, so why not us. You are not alone in this. You are alone if you decide to give up.

Here is how we gain back that control, but first I have to burst your bubble. If you think you can do this alone, you are sadly mistaken. You are going to need help, and depending on who or what you may feel you lost your control to, you might have to seek help from multiple sources. Professional help for some whether it's a psychiatrist/psychologist or a social worker.

Friends and family are suitable for a support system, but unless any of them has had the training in your particular need, then their help is limited.

I suggest seeking a spiritual Dr. I know a great one I could recommend, his name is God and it doesn't matter what's going on with you at any given time he has the remedy for it. You'll notice though the solutions all seems to be the same for any situation and that's to gives God control of your life. "Waite so to gain control of my life I have to give control over it to God where's the sense in that?" You may be saying.

When you give God control over your life, you have a sense of safety and excitement. "I don't want a sense of control I want actual control." you're saying, but do you really? How much more control do you think you'll get with God's help by giving total control of your life to God, you've just gained the ultimate control.

Think about it. With God in control of every aspect of your life, how bad can it genuinely get? Will everything be peachy? No. Will it be worth it? I say absolutely.

Have you ever read a bumper sticker that says God is my co-pilot? Think about that for a minute. A co-pilot is there to back up the pilot; take over in case something happens to the pilot right. Would it not make sense to have God as the pilot? You are guaranteed nothing can happen to this pilot, and all you have to do is check-in with him every day and know you have the best pilot in the world. How does that sound? Do you still want total control? I do not.

Ask yourself

1) *What or who have you given control to?*

2) *If you are the one, still in control, how are things?*

3) *Is the control you've lost caused by fear of losing control?*

4) *Have you sought help professionally or spiritually?*

5) *Are you ready to give control to god and make him your pilot?*

CHAPTER 15

I'mpossible

I'mpossible is not a misspelling or a trick phrase. It is a word I've been using to navigate and get through this world, which is a maze.

To change a negative to a positive does not require much skill. It does, however, takes practice and practice takes will.

"I'mpossible, it's not even a word you've just added an apostrophe to it." That may be so, but somehow that apostrophe is just the right fit.

You may find my thought pattern to be chidish or even laughable, all because I truly believe anything is possible.

To those who say I'mpossible is not proper English or acceptable jargon, new words are added every day, so drop your negative attitude and hop on the I'mpossible bandwagon.

After thought: Throughout our history, many things were thought Impossible and had been proven wrong by those who dared to think I'mpossible

The thoughts behind
I'mpossible

I'mpossible is one of those word play things I talked about in situations, but I cannot take credit for this word. I was made aware of the word I'mpossible back in the mid '90s, while volunteering for a nonprofit aids charity. They organized a 3-day bike trek from Boston to NY

Every year the organization would have some type of positive message that they would print on banners, stationery, basically, on everything that went out to riders, staff, and crew.

Now here is why I truly believe wordplay affects one psyche, especially mine. I was called into the office one day to help get out a 3,000 + pieces mailing. I naturally answered the call for help and went to the office. When I got there, I noticed the message for this year was impossible. I thought to myself well that is not very positive.

I sat down. I looked at the piles of letters that needed folding and stuffed into envelopes, then stamped, and I got overwhelmed. There were only three of us, how were we going to get this done?

It wasn't until I folded about 300 letters that I noticed this little mark next to the (I) of Impossible, so I tried to rub it off, but it didn't. I then thought it was a print defect. I said something to one of the other volunteers, to which they laughed and said, "it's an apostrophe." "The word is I'mpossible." Imagine how I felt.

You see, the mind sees what it wants to see, what I call the "norm." Even though the apostrophe in I'mpossible was in a different color, to make it stand out I couldn't see it. It did not make any sense to me at the time, so it had to be wrong. I am sure I am the only person has thought this way.

It was not until I started to look at the word for what its intentions were for did I notice a change in my thinking. I was more positive about the job at hand. I suggested ways to be more efficient. My attitude did a complete 180 degrees.

Once that happened I was aware of things that were not noticeable when I had the negative attitude, like the music that was playing the whole time, or the sweet-smelling perfume of one of the female volunteers was wearing. I began to talk and joke more with the other volunteers and staff. I'm happy to say that we got the job done. Even though it seemed impossible at first. It only took me to acknowledge that little apostrophe for things to become I'mpossible.

Ever since then I have taken the word I'mpossible at face value, I now always just insert that apostrophe and do what I need to do to make whatever I need happen. I have to be honest and tell you, I've given this word way more thought than you could imagine, or think one should. There was more to this word for me than just the positive thinking aspect of it, and it came to me soon after I started living in Christ again.

I started to remember the story of Moses, God chose him to free his people from Pharaoh in Egypt, and I remember Moses asking God "who shall I say sent me? When asked of your name, what shall I say to them?" You know or remember what God's response was? He told Moses to tell them, "I am who I am,"," he said "tell them that I am sent you." I can imagine Moses standing there scratching his head at this.

It was only through the power and grace of the "great I am" that made it possible for Moses to succeed. Do you see where I'm going with this? Time after time again, we can read throughout the bible that all things are possible through Christ Jesus if it is his will. Some may see this as a catch, but look at it from this point of view; our heavenly father only wants for us things that will lift him and each other. Why would he make it impossible if it is his will? Make no sense does it? Therefore, if we were to do God's will would it not make sense to be I'mpossible.

Furthermore, how many times have you had in your heart to do something you thought was a good thing, and you let people tell you how bad the idea really is or how impossible it will be, and you let them take up space in your head without paying rent? If you're like me, then you've lost count. Even though I had that I'mpossible attitude, I still had those who would try to discourage me, and put doubt in my mind. Thank God for giving me the strength to evict those thoughts and move forward. Who is your rebuttal voice?

I want to encourage you to take God up on his promises that all things are possible through him, for those who believe. Did you catch that other stipulation God threw in there? Believe, yes, you have to believe God will make a way for you to accomplish those things that are in line with his will. However, you can't just sit around and wait on Him to present it to you in a box with a bow. You still have to do some work for it. The next time someone tells you that what you are trying to accomplish in not possible, smile. Because you now know, it's a lie. Then tell them "that's what you think, but I'mpossible and let them stew on that for awhile.

Ask yourself

1) *Do I think anything is possible?*

2) *Do I feel you mentally insert that apostrophe and become I'mpossible?*

3) *Do I believe what I want for my life, is in line with Gods will?*

4) *Was there something I wanted for my life, but let others convince me that it was not possible? What are they?*

5) *Is this something I would still like to have? If so, am I ready to insert that apostrophe and go for it?*

CHAPTER 16

Given ups

Remember the days of old; playing, dreaming just having fun? Dreaming was a daily task, as a kid that's all that was asked. As you grew so did those dreams. How would I get them, by any means?

I've shared these with friends and family. Who often snickered, grinned and doubted me. I'm strong willed and determined to succeed, so get out of my way because here comes a dreaming stampede.

Dreams are falling like a storm of hail, how you dare you take the wind from my dreaming sails. A nice car, lots of money even the house on the hill. These are my dreams, not yours to kill.

When I dream that's when I fill most alive, so why do you feel so deprived? Success is what most people want, but instead of going for the home run, you just bunt.

What does success mean to me? " Success is the progressive realization of a worthwhile dream."(a quote by Dexter Yager)

To refuse to dream should be a sin

It is never too late to start dreaming again. Close your eyes and dream, it's not as hard as it may seem.

Who cares if you're an adult or a young pup? I'd rather be known as a dreamer, than a person who has just given up.

The thoughts behind
Given ups

Around the same time, I wrote the poem when I'm alone, I also wrote four other poems. They are the one you just read given ups, my bike and I, my life, and a Childs Dream, which you will read next. I only added three of them because they seem to fit with the theme of this book and because they are the only ones I could find after so many years passing since I've written them.

I wrote given ups when I was in my mid 20's and I was traveling a lot, doing some speaking engagements for organization; of which I was a member. Most of my speaking was for middle and high schools. I also did some colleges and community group.

What I loved most about doing these speaking engagements and what amazed me was these kids and many times teens' ability to dream, and I mean they put some thoughts into it. I loved the fact that they knew exactly what they wanted out of life. I found it so inspiring and it kept me dreaming.

I have seen many of these kids and teens years later in malls, movie theatres, or at my job. (At the time I worked for a sports arena) they were now grownups. After the initial greetings, I would question them about their success in achieving those dreams they spoke so adamantly about.

To my amazement, shock and some disappointment every one of them had similar answers. : oh I was just a kid then", "life happened", and this one kills me; "it just wasn't meant to be." These dreamers who have grown up to join the ranks of the many who I no longer call grown – ups, they have now become given – ups.

Why? Who stole their dreams? Who popped their inspirational bubbles? I'll tell you who. All of you people who have given up on your dreams. It's all the parents, who wouldn't support their children's dreams. It's the fault of those neighbors who said negative things about what they could achieve and who they could become. It's the fault of society for putting parameters around success and lastly all of you the dream stealers. Who have let your dream die? If you fall into one of these categories then I hope you have your hand raised.

If you have achieved your dream, but then stopped there, then you should have both hands raised, because no one put your dream fire out, you let it go out; and by doing so you stopped your inspirational affect.

I know you're a bit confused saying "what are you crazy? I didn't even know these kids you're talking of. How could I have affected their lives?" I'm glad you asked, cause and affect my friends, cause and affect; that's how. You see by giving up on your dreams or not establishing new aspirations you by default relinquished your ability to inspire, mentor, and teach the next generation.

Whatever your dreams were, who inspired them? Who planted that seed in your heart and mind? What would have happened if that person(s) gave up on their dreams? "Somebody else would have inspired me," you say. You think so well let us just see. Say your dream was to become a pro basketball player, now there are many teams in the league with many players on each team, but out of all these players there was that one; that one who caught your attention enough to make you want to play for the NBA.

There was just something about that player who inspired you to want to follow in their footsteps. What was it for you? Do you really think it could have been just any player to inspire you? I don't. That person who inspired you was all a part of God's plan for you. That same plan he's told us about, which was in place before we were conceived. So again, I ask you do you really think god would put just anybody in your path. I seriously doubt it

Everyone of us are a part of each other's plan, so when you give up or quit you are delaying or altering someone else's plan. "When is it too late to star dreaming again? You might be saying. Never, so go ahead and dream, but don't stop there go for them, achieve them, and keep dreaming. Remember this. Any and everyone have the right to give up on you, but you do not have the right to give up on yourself; God hasn't and he never will. Come on start dreaming, I dare you.

Ask yourself

1) *Are there dream I have given up on?*

2) *Did I let someone steal my dreams?*

3) *Am I willing to achieve some of these dreams still?*

4) *Am I willing to forgive them and move on?*

5) *If yes, what am I waiting for? If not; why not?*

CHAPTER 17

A Childs dream

Whether I'm born to parents who are young in age. I just want parents who aren't filled with rage.

It's not my fault that I am here, but now that I am, I'm your to care.

Nurture and love me is all that I long for. I'm your child for you to adore.

Mom and dad I will proudly call you. Through all your faults, I still embrace you.

mistakes will be made by day and by night, being mom and dad does not mean you'll always be right.

When I'm feeling down you'll be the first to know. Choose your words wisely, and be

Careful of what you say.

Remember you are my parents first, and then my friend, this is a statement I'll gladly defend.

This is also my recipe for a great family. It's also my dream for us to be.

this is dedicated to Maria/Jay P. In addition to all kids with young/angry parents. God is with you.

The thoughts behind
A child's dream

I have explained earlier when I wrote this, now it's time for the why. I wrote this poem for my little sister Maria T. Maria is not my biological sister, she is my sister from one of my many surrogate families. I had just found out that Maria was pregnant; she was only like 15-or 16 years of age. I have to admit I was a bit angry, not so much at her but more so with her family. I guess for them being so naive about her boyfriend situation.

It's funny because I think they knew I would be, since they tried to hide it from me. Little did they know I probably knew before they did? You see Maria and I were close for not being blood relation. I saw the changes in her; I saw the sign (yes I know that's a song as well). I'm not doing this on purpose I promise, but I did tell you I love music. Let us get back to Maria. She was the youngest girl in a family with eight boys and one other girl.

Maria cooked, cleaned and babysat far more often than she deserved to have. I personally think it ripped her of her childhood. It also made her a furious person. She was always yelling and screaming. You could hear her from down the street as you approached the house. This was her way of dealing with her family; there was seldom any low-level talk in her house. Some say it was their heritage, but I know it was more than just that.

Everyone yelled, struggling to get his or her points across. Maria was the main one yelling. Was she that bad? Yes it was and sometimes worse. Maria and I would talk about the situation from time to time. I told her I totally understand where she's coming from, and why it makes her angry, but just like it's not her fault she's put in this predicament; it is also not the fault of her siblings they were stuck with her as a babysitter. As you can imagine Maria did not like that at all.

Now Maria is not the only person I dedicate this poem to, she just happens to be the first. I'm very fortunate to have at least four surrogate families, plus my own biological and adoptive families except for my adoptive family all the others had someone in them that had anger issues. In some, it was an adult in other it was a child and both in some cases.

"Are you trying to say you don't get angry and yell Mr. cool, calm, and collected? You may not believe me, however if you asked anyone who knows me, if he or she has ever seen me angry or yell in anger, I bet they would be hard pressed to come up with a situation that they have. I don't say this to boast. I've just seen and heard so much of it; I've learned to channel it for myself. I've also seen the damage it causes and I don't want any part of that.

Here is my confession I do get angry and occasionally raise my voice, which is no shocker because everyone does. Come on now even Jesus got angry. What would I be suggesting if I said I didn't? Although Jesus did get angry, you would find it difficult to find many situations in which he did.

In the Bible, a verse starts with. "Be slow to anger." Easier said than done I know. In the poem, was a list of some scenarios that a child might face, and the reaction a child would like to see from their parents. I called it a recipe and as with all recipes there are multiple ingredients, but if you follow that recipe exactly you'll most likely end up with something most enjoyable.

I also said in the poem that being mom and dad does not always make you right. I bet that got under some readers skin. I said that because somehow parents think that title comes with all the answers or over compensate with authority with statements like; "because I said so."

There's only one parent who has all the answers, that is our heavenly father. So why put all that unnecessary pressure on yourselves? When a situation arise and your emotions begin to boil over, take a step or two maybe three back, then take a deep breath and count to a thousand if you have to. Don't sleep on it, deal with it that day, but for god sakes be very careful what you say and how you say it. Also, be very aware of what you don't say as well.

Look at it this way. What if God responded the way some people respond to their children, but also to people in general? Scary thought. Especially knowing how God dealt with people in biblical days. We don't have to worry about that now a days, because most people know he is a kind, loving, understanding and most of all a forgiving God. Knowing this of our heavenly parent, shouldn't our children expect this from their biological parents? It's not that hard to do and with practice, you'll get better at it. If this is what a child dreams of, here's your chance to make it a dream come true.

Ask yourself

1) Do I find myself yelling for no apparent reason?

2) Do I have an idea where the anger comes from?

3) Is it hurting my relationships?

4) Do I need to seek counseling for it?

CHAPTER 18

Life lessons

The life lessons that are learned are like confessions I am told, confessions that are revealed, as we grow old.

They are sometimes mistaken for memories or expressions. Sometimes it's not until we pass them, do we make the connection.

So keep your senses sharp, your eyes, ears, and most importantly your mind. To receive life's lessons of all kind.

Don't get caught up in all of life's torments, or you will surely miss many of lives ah ha moments.

Life lessons can be so profound; it is like being at a concert not able to hear a sound.

Everything will seem to slow down, and grab your attention. The truth be told that is life only mission.

There are life lessons in all we do. When you learn from them, they will become a blessing not only to you, but to all you teach them to.

Afterthought: "mistakes are life's lessons not yet learned" EK

The Thoughts behind
Life's lessons

Throughout my entire life, I've been blessed to have many amazing mentors and life coaches. They have shown and taught me many things, but I have noticed this one piece of advice they all had to share with me. The advice I got was to look for the life lesson in everything I do.

I took that advice to heart and ran with it. I started to actively search for the life lessons in everything I did. Some were obvious, while others were more evasive and I'm still just learning some.

When I did learn a life lesson, I always got excited to tell them to others, hoping to get them to search for life lessons of their own. Some people took up the challenge, and others didn't believe there could be a life lesson in everything we did.

My friends would sometime challenge me on this when we were participating in leisure activities such as eating at the restaurants or going to the movies. I am able to find the life lesson presented, my friends not so much. I believe it's because their minds were not open to seeing them or maybe they did and will acknowledge it later in life

There are some life lessons that we don't learn until many years later. How many times have you heard or said this? I wasn't sure what my parents meant by that until…" I've said it, how about you? Maybe for you, it was someone else, perhaps your grandparents, a teacher, coach or pastor. Perhaps it was police, a neighbor I don't know, but you do. I bet you'll always remember them for it I've learned a life lesson from everyone I just mentioned and a whole lot of other people in my life.

Sometimes the lessons can be ignored, forgotten, and misunderstood. A lesson not learned can cause mistakes over, and over again, hopefully until the lesson is learned.

In the past two and a half years, working on this book, God has introduced me to some more amazing mentors. Who have shared with me the ultimate life lessons; Gods words through the bible so what lessons have I learned? Well I've just shared with you 18 of them but let's recap.

In this recap, I'm going to reference some verses from the bible, but I want you to realize that those are just a few of the many verses you'll find throughout the Bible that is related to each topic I used to inspire each poem. Please don't stop at just the verses I referenced, do some research of your own, or go to your local church and talk with the pastor or elders. Now let us begin that recap.

In the book of John chapter 13 verse 13- 27, 'I've read about how Jesus was fiercely persecuted Because of who Jesus was and what he stood for, people hated him. In a way he was treated like a pariah; however, you wouldn't dare catch Jesus putting on a mask mentally or physically. Jesus accepted his calling and purpose, and he is proud of every one of us. Why else would he give his life to save ours?

In the book of Mathew chapter 11 verses 28 – 30, for those of you who are overworked and burdened, or just plain have a problem with life; in this chapter you find some solutions, and guess what? He offers it to us all. Do you want to know what some of those solutions are? You'll have to read it for yourself. I'll give you a hint, one of the solutions god offers is a give and take option.

When I'm alone nowadays I still think, but I now know I'm never alone. Reading Deuteronomy chapter 13 I am reminded of that. When I am lost in thought of what heaven is like I tend to read the book of revelations. Tell you this you read that and you'll get a clear picture of those thought.

some people really don't get the poem Orion's song, so I tell them to read the book of psalms chapter 42 verse 8 specifically. There the author of the book says, "That at night his song is with me" what song? Again, you'll have to read it to find out.

You can bet that the song is not by P. Diddy or Lady Gaga. Even still, I think if you could hear his song whatever it may be, you would agree that it would deserve a Grammy.

For those times when you feel or think you're better off by yourself, the bible is a great source of objections. Togetherness, unity and the call for us to be as one, is emphasized; all throughout the Bible. I especially love how psalm 133 starts off. It really gets me thinking. If God wanted us to be by ourselves then why would there be a need for twelve apostles? There are something's that are supposed to be, alone is not one of them.

In some Bibles, God's words are written in red. This is so the reader will know for sure the words were spoken by him. One word that I noticed a lot is the word now. This clearly mean at that moment, not in the future, but now. God definitely knows the difference between today and tomorrow. He created time; he also knows its better not to wait. Read Matthew chapter 6 verse 34, to get a better sense of how good feels about today versus tomorrow.

How's your relationship with God going? Not sure, is it because your too busy beeing a sojourner or a stranger like it says in psalms chapter 39 verse 12.well what are you waiting for? Are you waiting to find him? Remember he's not lost. Are you waiting for god to find you? Well you're not lost per say. He knows where you are. Gods just waiting for you to reach out to him; acknowledge him and accepted him. That way you are no longer a stranger to him anymore.

Jesus gave a new commandment in John chapter 15 verse 12. There he says to love one another. Jesus does not care what color we are, or how much money we have. There is no one better than Jesus who can truly look beneath the skin and see us for who we are, in fact Jesus looks deeper. He looks into our hearts and soul. Since we cannot do that, who are we to judge, James ask in chapter 4 verse 17.

In the book of Luke chapter 6 verse 21, Luke explains how as Christians we will still have hard times, but in the end, we will all laugh. Even now as Satan temps us, and tries to encourage us to keep sinning and to join his clan; god is in heaven shaking his head. Because god already knows who is going to have the last laugh. As the saying goes he who laughs last, laughs more.

In the first letter to John, John chapter 4 verse 20, John writes; if anyone says, they love the god, and hates his brother (brother meaning everyone and anyone) then they are liars. Strong words, don't you think? People need to stop lying to themselves and dial love – 911. Ask god to help them to love the right way, the way god intended for us to.

When you read the poem situations, I bet some of you thought I was blowing smoke. Well I'm not; an I'm also not the only person who feels this way about situations. To see what I'm talking about take a look at the book of second Kings Chapter 2 verse 19. (kjv) it is a great example of how your attitude can change your outlook on things, and make it just a situation where others see a problem.

Are you like me, do you feel too hard as my mother like to put it? Does it seem to get dark at noon for you sometimes? I have found someone in the bible who also felt that way his name is job. (Long o, not jahb like I use to say it) read his story in the book of job chapter 13, read the whole chapter in fact the whole book. Job describes exactly how I feel when I am around negative people, people who are in pain animals to for that matter. When I read this book I felt sorry for job, for what he experienced, his loss and how much he had to go through and how much he had to give up; well not really it was more like taken from him; all to test jobs faith. I am sure none of you feels like your faith is being tested. Your life is just peachy right. You'll have to read the story if you want to know how job faired, but the story in its self is a great life lesson.

You ever wonder why we are referred to as sheep in the Bible. It's because just like a Sheppard controls his sheep and leads them, comforts them and protects them; so does Jesus for us. I don't think the sheep have a problem with giving control to the Sheppard. I had no problem giving god control over me once I read psalms chapter 23. All throughout the bible, you'll read about the promises of god and I can receive them a lot quicker by giving him control of my life, because I'm on a mission to collect every single promise, how about you? You do not need to worry god does not break his promises only humans do that.

I'm concerned about the amount of people who have become given – ups. Therefore, I am going to let you in on a little secret on how to get what you want, if it's God's will. To unlock this secret read in the book of Matthew chapter seven verse 7. It's so simple that it only requires three things; ask, knock and seek. Does not make much sense now, but it will after you read it.

I gave you a look inside a Childs dream, and if you think about it, it's not much to ask for. You will be following Gods instruction as it is written in the book of Matthew chapter 18 verses 1-5, and your children will be happy to follow Gods commandment to honor thy mother and father, which is written in the book of Exodus chapter 20. In all of Gods ways, it is always a win, win scenario for all.

I told you there were life lessons in all we do and in the Bible. Those were just a few; there are tons more to learn just wait until you read the whole book, and I thank you for reading mine. Until next time my friends remember to live, love and laugh.

Ask yourself

1) *What life lessons was I told as a child, that I didn't learn until I became an adult?*

2) *Have I learned life lessons from places I didn't think was possible? What were they?*

3) *If I got paid $100 for every life lesson would I look for them everywhere and every day?(life lessons are priceless, so start looking)*

4) *Is there one life lesson I wished I would have learned earlier in life what would that be*

Epilogue

This has been an amazing journey. One that I came close to given up on, then as I read over the manuscript the poem given ups just kept speaking to me, and there was no way I was going to be that person. I'm so blessed to have God put people in my path that confirmed that this book need to be completed. My stories have to be told. Living a life of transparency is not the easiest thing I have chose to do, but we all know in doing anything worthwhile there will be challenges, that is what makes the victories even that much sweeter. I truly believe there is someone who have just finished reading this book and is now experiencing a life changing moment or an ah-ha moment, if this is you please contact me and let me through my email eokunmasking@yahoo.com

ACKNOWLEDGEMENTS

First, I have to thank God, for providing the situations in my life that I had to go through, and for all the experiences that inspired all of the poems. I also thank god for providing me with the words that I put into this book.

Second, I want to thank some people who whether they know it or not, have influenced and encouraged the writing of this book Deacon Ryan, Deacon J. O'Neal, and Pastor Hobbs and Pastor Wall of GMCC. Thank you for being my spiritual fathers. For taking the time to answer my questions and sharing the word of God with me, but most of all thanking you for showing me what true Christian work looks like.

To C. Leone, M Pepin, H. Vega, and J. O'Neil thank you all for inspiring those specific poems that made it into this book.

Thirdly, I want to thank all of my surrogate families: the Coppola's, Rober, Cheryl, Kris, Steph, Kim, the Tapia's, Elsa, Eric, Desiree, Kelvin, Irving, Maria and the Correa's Jason His Mom and Sisters. To all of my Christian family members. My love for you all knows no limits. Thank you!

To my biological family Michelle/Rochelle Kennedy, The Lockett's, and the Brown's/Green's. Although we have been apart for far longer than we have been together, it is those times together I will always cherish. I pray that God will continue to work on mending the wounds of the past, and bring us together again in the near future. I miss you all, and love you all dearly.

To all of my godsons who are now men: Dante Day, Deshawn Cross Day You have all been a blessing in my life. I'm so very proud of all of you. Thank you for helping me to realize what being a father would be like. Thank you Suan Day for your trust, friendship, love and support, I Can't wait to read your book one day.

To my best friend Jason Correa. thank you for always being there when I needed you most. True friends are hard to find, so thank you for being a true friend and most of all a brother.

I also want to give a huge shout out to a man who may not know it, but who I've always look to as a Father figure. He has also be a champion of mine, very encouraging and equally inspiring, Lenny Nelson; I love you dearly.

There are so many people I know I need to thank, so I'm going to just say if you at any point in time had any contact with me whether it was negative or positive; I thank you as well.